ESOT

THE OTHER SIDE

Maria Martinez
psychic medium

PAGE PUBLISHING, INC.
New York, NY

Publishing Coordinator: Jenna Amy
Cover artist: Maria Martinez

First originally published by Page Publishing, Inc. 2018

ISBN 978-1-64298-876-5 (Paperback)
ISBN 978-1-64298-877-2 (Digital)

Printed in the United States of America

Dedication

I would like to dedicate this book
to the following individuals:

Above all to God and my angels who watch over me,
my daughter, Patty, my Aunt Margie, my clients,
the spirits who talk to me,
and the future ones I have yet to meet.

Thank you. Blessings to all of the above.

Contents

Introducion

*M*aria Martinez, author of *7th Sense*, is the lead psychic in the book *Finding Aimée* by A. De Guerre.

She was born with the gift of a psychic, including the ability to talk to the dead and receive spirit message from the other side. While living in three dimensions, she has decided to take all the spirit messages she has received and present them to the world through this book, *Esoteric Poetry From The Other Side*. Some of these messages are their stories and pleas, while others are earthbound loved ones who are confused and lost, just trying to find their way home. Yet, there are a few who are trapped dark shadow spirits. Maria felt compelled to tell their stories, messages, and questions. She has encountered some of these stories personally with her own family's spirits and others with welcomed guests. With nothing but respect and love to all the spirits, Maria wanted to tell their messages in rhyme.

She is very close with the other side, so spirits have always found her. She loves them all! The most profound, beautiful, and loving spirit of Aimée, from the true story of *Finding Aimée*, is Maria's favorite spirit. Since meeting, Maria and Aimée have formed a special bond. Maria was very honored to be the lead psychic who finds out more about Aimée and her reason for being on this earth. She thanks A. De Guerre for giving her that chance.

Maria sends blessings to all who read these messages from spirits living on the other side. She urges you to try to understand their need to be heard and freed. Maria's messages are a collaboration between God, the spirits, and herself. You don't have to believe in something to understand it. Maria feels that we all share the same space; we're just in different dimensions.

Maria Martinez sends her blessings and wishes to say, "Welcome to my world."

Maria Martinez
714-539-9676

7th Sense of Meditation

Reaching the 7th sense of my soul,
Receiving messages new and old.

Meditating in travels to the other side,
Reaching souls that have long died.

Telling me their stories to write a poem,
Some are happy, others looking for home.

I am their messenger in poet both dark and light,
As they talk to me and share their life.

Thank you spirits, dark and light, for choosing me,
I'm humble and grateful and forever will be.

A Dream

Was it real, or was I dreaming?
I saw lights that were gleaming.

Beautiful and shining in gold and white,
So radiant in its luminous light.

I was in heaven with colors of gold,
Listening to stories that were being told.

Streets in heaven with angels of light,
Oh, so much to see, what a wonderful sight.

Then I awoke and opened my eyes,
Never to fear death again, I realized.

3:00 AM Call

Waking in the night, hearing the spirits call;
They love to make an entrance,
whispering in the hall.

Messages to share, stories they want to tell;
Some are from heaven and some are from hell.

They have no motive; they're just
looking for direction;
Trying at all times to get some love and attention.

Stories of sadness and stories of love gone away;
No memories of sound of night or day.

Spirits who seem to have lost their way;
Looking for the yellow sunshine's bright rays.

A Letter to Heaven

Dear departed family, I want to say hello,
To the ones that made it and the ones below.

Below I know that you can't read this,
Some of your names are not on the list.

But I wanted you to know I care,
Even though you're not up there.

So heavenly family and friends, I'll see you soon.
Meanwhile, I'll pray for the ones that are doomed.

Aboriginal Healer

He proudly sits on my wall in a painting;
Quietly anticipating a healing in waiting.

His colors so vibrant and wearing a headdress;
Always healing is what he does best.

Sometimes I walk by his painting on the wall;
I hear sounds and words of his native call.

I knew when I painted him, he was alive;
His spirit was active; I could feel his vibes.

Aboriginal healer ancient and wise;
Ask for a healing and never be denied.

A Merry Christmas Poem

'Twas the night before Christmas
with a double full moon,
Witches were flying on their Christmas-lit brooms.

The dark shadow people were
dancing through the halls,
As the other spirit orbs played
with the Christmas balls.

Hexes and spells at the stroke of midnight,
While the angels spread their wings
in their luminous light.

Pagans and shamans meditate in their prayer,
While ghosts and spirits are floating through the air.

Psychics, readers, palmistry, and such,
While others appear with a soft, gentle touch.

There lay a manger in a faraway place;
A baby was born with God's amazing grace.

So whatever you believe or to whomever you pray,
Always remember the true meaning
of Christmas Day.

Merry Christmas to all, and to all a good night!

A Ride to Heaven

As I closed my eyes, I found myself drifting.
I traveled through the light as my body was lifting.

I felt a presence like someone I knew.
I heard a voice but couldn't tell who.

"Oh, come with me and see the flowers of gold.
I'll share with you stories you've never been told."

I heard messages whispering in my ear.
I felt a peace that removed all my fear.

"I want to stay," I shouted out loud,
While my body was floating high on a cloud.

"No. No. You must go home
now. It's not your time."
As I awoke, I asked myself, "Was
this all in my mind?"

A Tiny Schoolhouse

They moved the tiny schoolhouse far away,
But the people said they still hear children play.

It was old and quite haunted,
And it was no longer wanted.

The teacher walks about the room,
Still teaching class and singing tunes.

No matter where the school house is,
They will always hear the laughter of kids.

A Wink in the Clouds

I dialed his number and asked by name.
A voice answered and said, "Is this a game?"

"He died quite a long time ago.
Who is this? Why do you want to know?"

I said, "I just talked to him the other day.
He called me and said he's far away."

When I talked to him on the phone,
He said he was all alone.

So later on that same day,
The phone rang in a mysterious way.

When I said hello, he let out a sigh.
Then he said, "I'm up here, look at the sky."

As I looked up beyond the sky,
I saw a wink in his eye.

Aura in Bloom

The dark shadow people with
your auras black as gloom;
Oh, witch pot perform your magic
on the next full moon.

Ask the gods to spare these souls
of colors not so bright;
Help them to find the path and
guide them to the light.

Shadow people born in darkness,
night became their friend;
Heal their souls from eternal hell,
and help this all to end.

Dark spirits of the night and
bright spirits of the day;
The force united together will
help them find their way.

Color me bright, oh aura, and bloom
rainbows within my soul;
And send your warmth; tell me
stories of the already told.

Descending to a higher power with
thoughts of colors so bold;
I can feel the glow and radiance;
it's warm and not so cold.

Aimée and Randolph

She appeared before my bedside with a glow.
I woke up just in time to say hello.

As she stood there staring down at me,
I asked her name, and she said, "Aimée."

I knew at that moment who she was:
An angelic angel filled with love.

She said, "Thank you for finding me,
And helping my soul to be free."

"I'm waiting for Randolph in my afterlife,
So I can be his bride and wife."

"Thank you," she said, "for guiding him to me,"
"And your psychic powers to help me see."

"Now my after life is no longer dim,
'Cause I'm so happy to be with him."

Aimée, Angel of Light

Sweet smell of rose myrrh, the
flowing dress within her light,
Her angel wings wide and glowing,
illuminating in the night.

Her beauty deep within her soul,
to protect us from fear.
Her mission in the afterlife, when
we need her to appear.

She illuminates the room and
gives hope in all despair.
Her spirit to be felt is more often than is rare.

Aimée, sweet child, with child
you passed way too soon,
I'll summon your love and
protection on all full moons.

Your beautiful earthbound energy
will always be here for me,
And that heavenly grace that you
possess I will always see.

Angel of light. Angel of night. I
know that you are here.
I see you now and feel your presence
as I watch you appear.

Thank you, Aimée!

All Aboard

Destination unknown; I'm just passing thru.
I don't know where I am; I have no clue.

Never been here; this is nothing I know.
Can you please tell where this ride will go?

"We don't know," cried a voice out loud.
"We're all here, lost souls in a crowd."

"We are all going to a different place.
Not all of us will travel at the same pace."

"Some will leave sooner; some will leave late.
It really all depends on our individual fate."

Angel on the Wing

They all boarded the plane late that night,
But bad weather detained their flight.

Then it was time for them to fly,
Straight through a rainy sky.

Then, the engine started to fail,
Because of a heavy falling hail.

Things were flying all around,
The plane was heading to the ground.

An angel was spotted sitting on the wing,
When someone heard the angel sing.

They landed safely and exited the plane,
The sun was shining with no more rain.

Command

It was a cold and foggy, dark night;
the streetlamps barely lit.
In the distant shadow, people were
walking while others just sit.

Looking for their home that once was there.
Walking around empty, needing someone to care.

Create them a path for they have no direction.
Shout and tell them with love and affection.

Light your candles, and sprinkle your dust.
Command your words with authority and trust.

Baby Shoes

A tiny boy drowned with his shoes on.
His spirit in those shoes still lives on.

His little shoes sit upon my shelf,
With sadness and memories heartfelt.

I freed the spirit to go to the light,
But he still visits me on certain nights.

I welcome his visit when he plays with his shoes.
He moves them around and separates the two.

He's happy now, both here and there.
I'll embrace his love, no matter where.

Baton Rouge Mystic

She sits in her dark gypsy room,
With a deck of cards on a full moon.

She is the Baton Rouge Mystic witch,
Who tells her stories in a deep vocal pitch.

Lots of messages to be received,
Some are troublesome and some relieved.

She's old and dark and lives all alone,
On Bourbon Street, in her home.

No bells to ring, no phone to call.
Just walk in, down a dark lit hall.

Eyes that pierce and a voice so low,
Some turn around, while others go.

Civil War Spirit

There was fire and heaven in his eyes,
As he had lived many lives.

Civil war fighter, front line battle,
Lost his life, blown off his saddle.

He told me his spirit could not rest.
"I'm looking for my wife; it's my quest."

"She died back home, while I was at war.
She was sick, and we were poor."

"Help me find her so I can rest."
Then, I said, "I'll do my best."

I summon her to come forward to me,
And there she was, where he could see.

They joined hands and walked away.
I still see their spirits to this day.

Clipped Wings

You clipped my wings so I couldn't fly.
My question is I want to know why.

To control my will or to possess my soul?
You show no warmth just callused and cold.

My wings will grow back in future time.
A time to fly away, I know I will find.

If not, then maybe with heaven's wings.
Then I'll be protected by many kings.

The Portal Lovers

As they traveled through the portal light,
Longtime lovers steal the night.

They always travel and come in two's,
With the colors of blue hues.

They appear at night when it's dark,
Always together and never apart.

They embrace in the portal light,
Making love all through the night.

They can only reveal themselves this way,
Because their spirits aren't here to stay.

Doggie Cemetery

While cremating my dog, I walked around;
Hearing the barks and howling sounds.

I visited graves of loved ones' souls;
Some were young; others were old.

When suddenly I looked and saw them playing;
I realized they were no longer lying.

Happy and running around the graveyard;
Barking and rolling and playing real hard.

I knew just then they do have souls;
Dogs and cats, both young and old.

Country Dream

When I come back, I have a country dream.
To live where the stars talk and the air is clean.

No more city lights, fast pace, or loud sounds.
I died too young in the street city town.

Someone with a gun shot me in the head.
Upon arrival, I was pronounced dead.

I told my God when I return,
The city life I have learned.

Please send me to a safe country place,
Where life is a much slower pace.

I'm ready now; I have paid my dues.
When on earth, a death I did not choose.

Dance with Your Demons

May I have this dance? Yes, you can!
The sooner I get to know you, the better I am.

Ignore your demons, and watch them grow.
They will all line up straight in a row.

Taking over your thoughts and desires.
They are very deceiving and good liars.

Taming your soul and watching you die.
Filling your dreams with nothing but lies.

So dance with your demons; know how they move.
You have much to gain and less to lose.

Deep into the Ocean

My shoulders are hurting. Am I afloat,
or am I deep into the ocean?
I see the bubbles and hear the water,
as I descend deep into the ocean.
My eyes are closed as to not see the
direction, as I go deep into the ocean.
I float in an oblivious state of consciousness,
as I go deep into the ocean.
Who's there, or is the mind playing
tricks, as I go deep into the ocean.
No smell, no human life, and no cars,
as I go deep into the ocean.
Mama, can you hear me? I'm calling.
Or are you deep into the ocean?
Suddenly, I see a bright light. I'm ascending
now as I go deep into the ocean.
I reach for the surface with no breaths
of air as I go deep into the ocean.
I feel the sand beneath my feet. Is this
shore land or deep into the ocean?
My eyes finally opened, and I realized it was
just a dream of being deep into the ocean.

Dialing 666

You have reached hell; we can't take any calls,
As we are surrounded by fire and big walls.

I can't reroute your call to another dimension.
I'm in lock down and doing my detention.

I'll be unavailable and never able to leave,
Because my life on earth was a venomous weave.

If you misdialed, please hang up the phone.
Then dial 0 for God; He'll redirect you home.

His Muse

Tall and beautiful with raven-black hair.
Eyes that pierced you with her stare.

His muse, his love, and his sexual desire.
Her clothing, her smell, and his diviner's attire.

Forever his muse she shall remain.
Always to love in purity, not in vain.

Their souls will remain together in the hereafter.
Sometimes, I can hear them engaging in laughter.

Floating Sinking

My intoxicated soul is floating in a
dimensional space of nowhere.
Festally sinking in an upward motion
in a world without a care.

I'm sinking down by request, but
to stop somewhere midway.
The light is dark. The dark is bright.
Is this night, or is it day?

Sideways, upward, and around the
square. I feel I'm floating down.
Take me into your parlor so I can
feel the earthy ground.

One step, two steps. I'm almost
there, going upward bound.
Hold my hand gently; take me to
a place I once had found.

I'm going home far away from
this floating sinking ride.
Help me find my way from here,
a place where I once died.

So lost and confused, I'm looking
for that place called home.
The spirits of another world really
never seem to be alone.

Flying Lessons

Look at me I finally got my wings
today. I hope I can fly.
So strange to think I couldn't get them until I died.

It took me a long time to earn
respect to get my wings.
I had to obey all the laws and
stand before many kings.

Oh, mamma, are you proud? I was given such a gift.
My wings are white as pure snow
and are a perfect fit.

They light up like magic upon my halo frame,
And they protect me from bad weather and the rain.

The beauty and the purity in all its glowing essence,
But mamma I can't fly my wings;
I need flying lessons.

Mamma I want to fly my wings
so I can come to visit you.
Oh, child, you're here with me; I
thought you already knew.

Four-Leaf Clover

Can I make a wish with a leaf missing?
Will my wish still come true?
You told me four leaves don't matter,
as long as the leaves are new.

I held the clover to my heart and
wished good thought of you,
But then I looked and realized
the leaves only had two.

I can't find a four-leaf clover. Not one, two, or three.
Oh, here is just a steam, so I'll make a wish for me.

I don't need a three-leave clover to
make my wish come true.
I just remembered I have a magic pot
to make wishes brand-new.

So I put all the clover leaves in
my magic pot of gold,
And when I looked again, all the
leaves were four unfold.

The magic is within your soul
and whatever you believe.
It gives back and will grant you
all your wishes and needs.

Ghosts in the Basements

The old house was closed down.
Everyone knew why in town.

Rumors of screams and visions of ghosts,
Among other things a variety of hosts.

I visited that old house in town,
Right before they tore it down.

Spirits begging for direction and hope,
While I was summoning them and trying to cope.

I told them get out, go to your light,
With holy water, sage, and a fight.

They did not want to leave that day,
So all I could do then was to pray.

Suddenly, a soft wind blew,
With a light of a beautiful hue.

The spirits rejoiced as they flew away.
I knew God would never let them stay.

Lady in White

Your aura of light reflecting on the waters.
The legend of your spirit among
the ship of boarders.

As you wander the boat in a dress of pure white,
Rumors about you traveling to your wedding night.

Waiting for your love to exchange
the marriage vows.
Something happened, you disappeared
from the ship's bough.

Your spirit still haunts the boat to this day.
I know because we sort of met in a way.

Gotta Smoke?

A cold, damp ally with bodies on the ground,
Sleeping like animals in a lost and found.

Homeless and hungry without a dime to their name,
Asking "Gotta smoke, sir?" without any shame.

Waiting to become spirits of darkness in the night,
While others are holding on to
what's left in their life.

The stale smell of flesh, death waiting in the wing,
While the angels protect, comfort, and sing.

Hall Pass

I want to visit my loved ones I
left behind that I miss.
I want to hold them once more
and leave them with a kiss.

I see them every day and protect them with my love.
I look down upon them from the clouds high above.

I touch them in their sleep as I
stand beside their bed,
Feeling more alive when with
them than feeling dead.

Protect them from harm and all evil dark and gray.
Wishing good thoughts while casting the bad away.

My privilege that I've earned my visits that will last.
"I paid karma," said my prayers,
"to receive my hall pass."

So empty your soul, and fill it
with future love and peace.
Then you will earn your stars with
God and not with the beast.

Hello Again

I heard your voice in whisper and
felt you there last night.
I reached out to touch you as you
came through the light.

Oh, beautiful spirit, as you are
somewhere in my thought.
Our time was short; we knew love
and shared heart lessons taught.

Soul mate of the universe and love of many things,
An angel in heaven to protect me
under your special wings.

Come back and stay next time
around; I'll be waiting for you;
Or let us journey together now
and start our lives as new.

The sweet smell of magnolia and roses all in bloom.
I know I'll see you and talk to you
with the next full moon.

Hearts on fire, souls adrift in other dimensions away.
But I can close my eyes to see
you yesterday and today.

Many Rooms

My house has many rooms,
Filled with spirits all in bloom.

Some are related, others unknown,
Always welcome to visit and roam.

No spirit is a stranger in my many rooms.
People who visit don't fear just assume.

They know my house of many rooms,
Also has witches flying their brooms.

You will fear what you don't know.
Learning their magic will help you grow.

Kindred Souls

I loved you more than a brother,
And never less than no other.

You took your life and a piece of me.
I tried to help with what I could see.

I couldn't win the fate card that you held.
You were finished here and so compelled.

I know you in spirit as I knew you in life.
I feel your presence, and I see your light.

You shine it down upon me when I'm asleep.
That light goes through me so heartfelt and deep.

Hourglass Love

A love so fast, seems like one hour is all we had.
You were taken way too soon, and
my heart remains sad.

Fairness not at all as we feel it slipped us by.
So many questions with no answers I ask why?

Somewhere in time we will finish out our lives,
Or can it be possible that the hourglass lied?

Perhaps the sand in the bottle was moving very fast.
Then the hands of time can be
brought back into the past.

I Birth You Twice

When I held you and looked into your eyes,
There was a strong resemblance but in disguise.

I know we have done this before.
We both time traveled through that door.

You came back into my life once more.
I know we're soul mates to the core.

You were taken from me way too soon,
Before you could even grow and bloom.

I'm thankful for the new life we share,
A mommy with lots of love and care.

I Heard You Calling

I heard you calling, but I couldn't see you.
When I reached to touch, there was something new.

Far removed and gone like the season,
Or did we stay for the wrong reason?

I watched you grow like a seedless flower.
I was yours, you were mine, and we were ours.

Time in a bottle like the tic of a clock,
Or is it a key to my heart without a lock?

I gave you something, or did you take it back?
I see all good things white; you see them black.

I feel with my thoughts and see with my heart.
I think with my love and hear we're apart.

Can this be magic, or is it just a dream?
Like the props in a theatre, can we change the scene?

It's like the words to a song all in reverse.
Were we really listening, or did we just rehearse?

I'm leaving now, but somehow I can't see you.
Open your eyes; then maybe you can see me too.

I'm at the Gate

I'm at the gate; please let me in.
I've paid my karma and repented my sin.

Please open it so I can see,
If someone's there waiting for me.

I have nowhere to go from here,
Just my soul that's full of fear.

Hear my cry for help I yell.
I have already been to hell.

I had many lives many times,
And have committed several crimes.

Are you there, or did you leave?
Please don't leave me here to grieve.

Am I not worthy to step inside?
Please open that gate; open it wide.

My Best Friend

I saw your face; I looked into your eyes.
They told me a story with little left to hide.

Some words unspoken and secrets left to share,
A sound in your voice, a song sung with care.

Windows to the soul, some sadness of yesterday,
Exchanging words of wisdom with
thoughts that will stay.

Tomorrow will come and so will the light.
What follows thereafter is still out of sight.

For now in the moment, we share our time,
Cause true friends together are precious to find.

Incoherence

The will is weak; the mind is strong,
But it makes the heart choose wrong.

Never to hear the wind ringing the bells,
And only knowing the stories that he tells.

Walking in the dark without the moonlight,
Sunshine gone, there's nothing in sight.

Has my mind weakened to a thoughtless task,
Or encourage my will and create a new path?

Inner Voice

Inner voice, I heard you talk, but I didn't listen;
Every time I don't I learn a new lesson.

Inner voice you are my protection,
And your messages are always to perfection.

What spirit do you share within me,
One that hears or one that sees?

Wisdom messages so profound and true,
From now on I will listen to you.

Mamma, Can You Hear Me?

I had to leave; the angels called;
they took me far away.
I didn't want to go with them; I
wish I could have stayed.

Mamma, can you hear me; I miss
your hugs and kisses.
I'm right here with you now to
grant you all your wishes.

Don't just see me in your dreams;
look; I'm right there.
I love you and I see you; I'm your angel in despair.

Smile for me, Mamma, and I'll send you some light,
All in different colors that are beautiful and white.

Gotta go, Mamma, my time is up; I'll see you soon,
Or maybe when your lonely just
look up at the moon.

I'll be looking back at you with a twinkle in my eye.
Always know this is the beginning
and never a goodbye.

Her Nemesis

He was not an angel, not even close,
Angry disposition, a cold-hearted ghost.

He came to her in afterlife, the same as he was here,
With bad intentions and dark shadows, he appeared.

She still loved him in her suffering and pain,
Knowing all along she had nothing to gain.

Her nemesis was her dark side,
And her love she couldn't hide.

She couldn't change her path of destruction,
As she was under his spell of abduction.

Old Strega Witch

She's old and wise in secret disguise,
And gives you the answers with just her eyes.

Aged with wisdom, hunched over and brittle,
She gives nothing straight, only in riddle.

Mumbles with gestures, never a clue,
All the answers and thoughts are up to you.

Old Strega Witch lady, strange and sly,
Always tells the truth and never the lie.

Letting Go

I never meant to hurt you by leaving so soon.
I'm letting go and moving on, leaving my cocoon.

Going to a faraway place to meet the ones I miss.
I'll always be back to visit and leave you with a kiss.

My body is tired, and my mind is
gone like an empty shell.
Staying here and holding on would be a living hell.

As I kneel to my master, he shall guide the way.
My soul will rejoice, and my karma will be paid.

Love for Sale

She's alluring and beautiful with memorizing eyes,
As she walks the streets of corruption and lies.

A soul adrift still going through all the motions,
A pocket of money to buy more love potions.

The stale smell of perfume she wears in the night,
With her black silk stockings and a skirt worn tight.

She's looking for peace in that hereafter place,
Not realizing her death she has not yet faced.

She tells me her stories and sad words of sin,
And all her regret of the night secrets within.

Old Haunted Ship

His spirit remains locked in his room,
On the old haunted ship parked in a lagoon.

I saw him when I visited his room.
He touched my shoulder night of a full moon.

He shouted, "Get out; no one's welcome here,"
And with that, he did appear.

I visit that ship quite often now,
But never to visit his room I vowed.

I respect his spirit that died in that room.
I just hope he finds peace on that lagoon.

Old Magic Shoes

Old magic shoes, what path shall I take today?
Guide me to a place where I can stay.

All I have are theses magic shoes,
So many roads that I can't choose.

I have left everything I own behind,
And now I'm somewhere else in time.

These magic shoes old and worn,
Have been through many storms.

Take me through just one more time,
So I will know that path to find.

Redemption

Listen to me; I'm yelling; can you
help me find my God?
No color nor creed matters to
me; lift me from this fog.

I just can't see Him or Her or Whomever it shall be.
Whom do I confess my sins to now if I can't see?

No need for eyes, ears, or words.
Confess within, and you will be heard.

A God so powerful, forgiving, and wise.
Will always appear real, never in disguise.

No

No eyes to see, no ears to hear, and
no mouth to say what's mine.
No heart to feel, no feet to walk,
and no clock to tell the time.

No power in my world not even
in theirs can I see through.
No words or language can I speak
or songs to make me blue.

No, I don't exist in this world; I
just visit from time to time.
No, I can't stay very long, just for
a moment that I can find.

No pain within my being or sad feelings to regret.
No cares to worry about the things
I welcome to forget.

No place other than my existence do I care to be.
No earth nor hell nor heaven, just
a feeling of being free.

No color to decide or what day I need to choose.
No right or wrong decisions made to win or lose.

Old Haunted Phone

Spirit calling on an old haunted phone,
When not plugged in, just standing alone.

The dial moved slowly on its own,
As it made an annoying rickety tone.

Spirits trying to connect to the other side,
Sometimes even long after they have died.

Them needing comfort in hearing a voice.
You don't have to answer; you have a choice.

Phantom Mania

Oh, spirit of dark and demonic dimension,
Release yourself from your bad intention.

I command you to leave; you have not won,
In God's holy name, the Father, and His Son.

Anointing my body with protection and prayer,
Against all that's possible with a spirit in despair.

Phantom mania spirit, the most evil of dark,
Working so hard to leave your demonic mark.

Radio Tower

An old man worked in the radio tower;
Sat there day after day, hour after hour.

Listening for voices and hearing odd sounds,
And not ever aware they were spirit bound.

"Hello," he would shout and call out his name;
Every day he would play the same game.

Then one day, a voice came through,
And said, "Hello, I know you."

The old man answered and said, "Who are you?"
"It's me," said the voice, "someone you knew."

"I'm your brother; I'm happy you finally found me."
Old man said, "My brother is dead; this cannot be."

"You've contacted heaven; that's my new home,
And you reached me through the radio tones."

Sitting Angels

Beautiful angels sitting all in a row,
Waiting to see where they will go.

Flying with their brand-new wings,
Making magic and all kinds of things.

Hoping to find some souls in waiting,
With confused thought and debating.

Giving them guidance in their new path,
Praying for their death to come fast.

Old Wicker Chair

On the porch sat an old wicker chair,
That rocked back and forth with no one there.

People claim they see his spirit,
Some say he still sits in it.

The house sits empty except for him,
He won't leave to be with his kin.

I've seen that house and the chair,
I know that he still lives there.

He said to me, "I'm here to stay."
"It's been my home since back in the day."

Portal Vortex

You make your entrance through beautiful light,
A portal or vortex in day or night.

Colors from other dimensions
with the scent of myrrh,
Whom once lived here and roamed the earth.

Powers we cannot understand or possess,
Not until our souls are put to rest.

Work your magic through prayer meditation,
Relax and take deep breaths; be patient.

And maybe while you're still here,
The angels will teach you how to steer.

Sea of Mysteries

She liked to visit and sit high on the cliff,
Way above the sea, watching the waves drift.

The sea was angry on that day,
And a huge wave took her away.

She disappeared from that cliff,
Until they found her body adrift.

Many souls there lost their lives,
From the angry, high rip tides.

She died a famous artist and very young,
Old down town is where her paintings are hung.

Separated Twins

We arrived way to soon before our time.
Her death came fast; her soul I still pine.

We shared the womb and motherly love.
I know she's in heaven with angels above.

"Where are you?" I ask all the time.
Why is the answer so hard to find?

I want the answer, why did I survive?
When she is dead and I'm still alive.

An angel appeared and said to me,
"God made her an angel, forever to be."

Sleep Paralysis

I lay awake in my slumber, feeling
numb and confused,
Hearing a voice talking while my
body is being abused.

Taking away my breath and
holding me against my will,
As I lay partially awake, defenseless, quiet, and still.

My inner voice screams out in terror and delusion,
While trying to collect my emotions with confusion.

A spirit bound to control me in my defenseless state,
As I lay there in prayer and silence, awaiting my fate.

I awoke to see nothing, just felt a cold chill,
From spirits in the night that hold
you against your will.

Rose Petals in a Jar

Anniversaries, birthdays, and special love days,
Rose petals in a jar that just sit and fade.

Traces of memories all from the past,
Some stayed long, while others didn't last.

Colorless petals with no sent to smell,
Stories of love while others from hell.

Rose petals in a jar I free you now,
Of lost promises and broken vows.

Go into the wind and fly far away,
Maybe love again, maybe someday.

Something Remembered

A ring on your finger or a picture from the past,
A moment to be remembered or a feeling to last.

A song with no words or a scent of bloomed flowers,
A journal with no pen or a memory filled hour.

A face with a smile or a thought with a frown,
An old, tattered wedding dress or a missing crown.

A tear filled with joy or a tear filled with pain,
A lifetime of years or a book filled with fame.

A place of peace or a piece of a place,
A journeyed path or a stumbled pace.

A choice to make or a choice to take,
A destiny made or a dream to fake.

Stars Crossings

Shining star falling from the sky.
We stopped to kiss as you flew by.

Kismet timing for star-crossed love,
With angels singing high above.

Oh, shiny stars, twinkling light,
Falling in love in the dark of night.

So when you wish on a falling star,
Your true love will know who you are.

Stars Only Shine When It's Dark

Fear not the night because it's dark.
The stars will guide you to a new start.

The dark sky is a beautiful sight,
As the stars shine in their light.

Stars don't shine in the day,
Nor in the sunshine rays.

Only at night to wish upon a star,
So the gods will know who you are.

Tea Leaves

She drank the tea and waited awhile,
Until the leaves settled into a pile.

She turned the cup upside down,
And read the leaves she had found.

Strange messages were coming through,
She said, "I see many spirits with you."

Some are sad, and others are lost,
Then more leaves she had to toss.

Upon my leaving her that day,
I now drink tea a different way.

Thanks for Calling

"Hello. This is heaven. How may I direct your call?"
"I would like to only speak to my mom. That's all."

"Oh, I'm so sorry, but she's unavailable at this time.
She's looking for all the new
spirits that she can find."

"Can I please take a message? I'll send it to her soon.
I'll see her tonight as we all gather
for the full moon."

"Tell her I miss her every single day and night,
And give her a kiss when you hug her tight."

"I'll be there tonight looking at the moon,
As I know we'll be together again someday soon."

The Altar

She walked down the aisle,
To be wed in beauty and style.

He died last night while asleep,
All she could do was weep.

He said meet me at the altar tonight.
We will marry in the full moon light.

Marry me in spirit and soul,
And together we will grow old.

At the altar he whispered in her ear,
And down her cheek ran a tear.

The Astral

As I lay in my helpless body, floating
above against my will,
Everything around me feels lifeless,
cold, stale, and still.

I reached for the light but to no
prevail could I succeed,
For I was certain at that moment
this was all that I need.

A voice whispered in my ear and
said it's not your time to go.
You have much unfinished and many
seeds that you must sow.

You are too young and beautiful
and not ready at this time,
And at that point, I knew my soul
had agreed with my mind.

I descended back into my body as
I viewed my life in thought,
With gratitude and humbleness
an experience well taught.

When the gods want your soul, they'll
come like a thief in the night.
They will guide you with the truth and
show you the way to the light.

The Automatic Writer

He said I was famous when I lived here.
I wrote through spirit without fear.

He told of events that were happening,
While the pencil in his hands tapping.

I have no control where the pencil goes.
It glides across my paper it only knows.

He scribbled a message meant for me.
So I was the only one who could see.

It said I am your special spirit guide.
Here, take the pencil and watch it glide.

The Beating of the Drums

He sits on my shelf, vintage and old,
Drumming his stories of the untold.

Native and dark skin from another land,
Catching him often drumming with his hand.

Sounds in the quiet night while deep asleep.
He drums on his drum to a mysterious beat.

Voodoo doctor drumming his sound,
Healing the natives of his hometown.

The light of energy and sound of a song,
With its whimpering haunting all night long.

The Beggar

He was cold in tattered clothing
with a look of deep despair.
He looked me in the eye and asked,
"Do you have change to spare?"

I reached down into my pocket
and found a dollar bill,
But when I extended my hand,
it left me with a chill.

When I handed it to him, he
disappeared before my eyes.
Perhaps I'm being tested from an angel in disguise.

They come in sheep's clothing, both poor and alone.
No food, no money, just in rags,
souls without a home.

Always count your blessings by
the grace of God go I.
I will never ever forget that despair look in his eyes.

The Bridge

I was very confused and depressed.
I wanted to put my sadness to rest.

I prayed to my God to please forgive.
I can't go on; I don't want to live.

Don't judge me for this mistake.
My life is what I'm about to take.

I got high up on the bridge.
Standing straight up on the ledge.

Suddenly, I heard a voice that said,
"Please don't jump, you will be dead."

"Come down, I love you, it's not time,
For I am your God, and you are mine."

The Childless Man

I can't find my child since I've been gone,
Just her old doll that keeps me holding on.

A doll she loves my spirits attached to,
In hopes that it keeps me close to you.

I'll be waiting for you in the hereafter.
I can see you, and I can hear your laughter.

Late at night when you're deep asleep,
I stand beside you and sometimes weep.

My precious child, so young and pure,
A soul I will love and always adore.

The Crystal Ball

Oh, crystal ball, haunted and old,
Has many stories to be told.

Look deep into the ripples of glass,
While I work my magic spell cast.

A wish to be granted, a questioned asked,
With words easily spoken never a task.

Then one day, the crystal ball fell,
Into so many pieces one couldn't tell.

A new crystal ball appeared one day,
In a very mysterious kind of way.

The Dark Man

He comes in the night dressed
like an angel in disguise.
He'll suck away your breath as
he gazes into your eyes.

He's powerful and determined to
take control of your soul.
He is both beautiful and ugly
and warm and also cold.

He will mesmerize all your thoughts
without your permission.
He cheats, he lies, he takes, and he
is capable of your submission.

He's dark, he's light, and he's everything
both in lust and in passion.
He's clever, he's bold, and he bravely
works best when he's in action.

He neither sleeps nor cares; his euphoria is you.
He has a wisdom that's profound
and a personality to woo.

"Beware," I say with wisdom, "do
not look him in the eyes."
He comes as many faces and his clothing in disguise.

The Doorbell

It's broken; it doesn't ring anymore.
It just sits there on the door.

And then it made a funny sound.
When I looked, it had fallen to the ground.

The haunted clock chimed twelve times,
While the broken doorbell sound in rhymes.

"Who's there," I asked with no reply,
As a long time had gone by.

Finally, I opened the door to look,
And saw the doorbell back on the hook.

I pressed it once to make it chime.
It was for sure broken this time.

I closed the door and walked away.
Then again, I could hear the chimes play.

Oh spirit what message do you convey?
When I saw a shadow walk away.

The Embryo

It was a special star that shined, oh, so bright.
It came down from heaven to create a life.

Floating in a stream of love, it
found a nesting home.
Knowing that I was safe and never more to roam.

Moving in a circular motion in
my embryonic sound.
Feeling like this is my home
somewhere new I found.

I'm attached to you for now; I'll slumber for a while,
And in nine months to come, you will birth a child.

A child of love and comfort to be a part of you,
On that beautiful day, our one will become two.

The Empty House

The old sounds from the walls of kids playing
As the spirits left behind remain staying.

Houses that can tell stories of the past
Lingering scents and vibrations that last.

Building new memories for future thoughts
Of this empty house that I just bought.

So don't fear the spirits that were left behind
You are all sharing the same house; try to be kind.

The Fairview St. House

Her spirit still roams the Fairview St. house.
I have reason to have no doubts.

She wandered the house all about,
As we watched her walking in and out.

She played with the children late at night,
Making sure their blankets were nice and tight.

Then one day, as she crossed the hall,
Her daughter saw her, and she called.

"Mama, I can see you; is that you,"
Not knowing really what to do.

I know that house very well,
With a lot of stories I can tell.

I lived there after my grandma passed.
I have many memories that will last.

The Flame Reader

She lit the candle and looked at the flame,
Called upon a spirit by its first name.

"Spirit of fire, what is your message today?
Please tell me what you have to say."

The spirit flickered the flame real high,
And before it spoke, we both heard a sigh.

The spirit said, "Pray to the moon tonight,
The message will come through its light."

She prayed later to the moon that night.
The spirit was there, and the message was right.

The Grandfather Clock

Old and ornate clock with hidden haunting sounds,
Sending out messages when the clock was wound.

Deep words in despair, dark-sounding noise,
Some words were negative; others were wise.

Old haunted clock with your spirits all aglow,
Telling your stories night after night all in a row.

I did give you away to someone loved and dear,
You spirit was gone, so your words he didn't hear.

I miss you old, grandfather clock of dark and gray,
I'm sorry, please forgive me for giving you away.

The Haunted House

"Get out," he said, "I live here,
you're invading my home."
He sits in the window everyday
by himself, there all alone.

He haunts the staircase hall and
rooms every day and night,
Plays with bells, bangs on the walls,
and turns off the lights.

"Old man, go away, find your place far from here."
"The light is looking for you,
go into it without fear."

"I live here with my family, this is not your home."
"Go to your loved ones now, and
never more to roam."

The Hitchhiker

Beautiful dead spirit roaming the street,
Searching for home with no shoes on your feet.

Ragged clothes of many years gone by,
Never to realize that you have died.

Hitching home on a dark lonely hill,
In hopes you'll find that void to fill.

With child innocence searching for home,
Never to mutter a sound or even a tone.

The Inheritance

To my beautiful daughter, I leave you my heart,
So I know that we're never far apart.

To my wonderful son, I leave you my eyes,
Always to watch over you as time goes by.

My friendship I leave to my best friend,
Knowing we'll be together till the end.

My wisdom I'll keep tight in my urn,
'Cause that is something you have to earn.

The Inn

On the top of a hill stood the old dark inn,
Shabby and haunted with a roof made of tin.

The willow trees whistling their sound,
A dense fog with moss on the ground.

A shabby dark door leading into the inn,
No sound or lights, just dark and dim.

A bell sat on the desk with an old book to sign,
So old and ragged from another place in time.

The smells of musk and darkened days,
As the old inn spirits are there to stay.

The Jar on the Mantel

My ashes sit on the mantel alone,
In a place I use to call home.

I want to be set free to fly,
Not in a jar when I die.

Take me somewhere far from here,
Where music plays and there's no fear.

Blow all my ashes to the sea,
And then I know I will be free.

Don't keep me here for the wrong reasons,
I want to fly among the seasons.

I want to be released from that jar,
Please allow me to visit the stars.

The Lake

It holds a mysterious haunting
the whispers about town,
No one really knowing who or
exactly how many drowned.

The lake was dark and murky with
many souls beneath the water,
Men, women, children, someone's
son, and someone's daughter.

The lake was cursed with tragic
death, the souls of many lost.
Killed then dispossessed of and into
the lake they were tossed.

It's still a mystery, and it may never come to light,
All the dead souls that were killed there that night.

The Magic Pillow

Dreams of other places in time,
Looking for roads I never find.

Always lost somewhere far away,
Looking for a place to stay.

Faces I don't even know,
Places I don't want to go.

Oh, magic pillow, take me home,
So in my sleep I'll no more roam.

Maybe it's the pillow where I lay my head,
Or is it this old haunted broken down bed?

The Messengers

Oh, spirits of the universe with
messages so profound,
I hear you, and I see you both in sight and in sound.

No hour of the day nor a warning to be told,
You come upon us in spirit strong and gently bold.

Who is your intelligence of a higher god to praise,
Or is this just simply something of that like a maze?

To claim these powers means to define who you are,
Oh, spirits of the other side so close and yet so far.

Behold in amazement; I give to you a higher grace,
Your energy is much too sacred in
this shared divided space.

Dimensions apart yet always ready to be at hand,
With respect and admiration, I
continue to understand.

The Middle

I've not gone up but neither down.
I just seem to be hanging around.

I feel like I'm still here with you.
I'm not really sure of what to do.

I want to stay I'm afraid to leave.
I'm earthbound watching you grieve.

Release me now, and stop holding on.
I'll still be here even though I'm gone.

The Morgue

Cold and lost voices yelling, "Hey, I'm over here,"
Laying on slabs in their death with fear.

Let me out; I want to fly and be free,
I want to talk, hear, and be able to see.

"Who's there?" said the keeper in a deep voice,
"It's us, and we're here without any choice."

When I die, don't put me in there,
Just spread my ashes everywhere.

The spirits' messages were so profound,
Please don't bury me into the ground.

The Nuptials

The road was dark and drenched with rain.
We were driving in hopes of nuptials to exchange.

Excited with joy, we were driving too fast.
It took our lives going over the pass.

Now both in spirit, we want that vow,
But we're not sure exactly how.

Please help us to complete our lives.
We want to take the nuptial ties.

On a full moon night, I will summon you,
And perform the vows between you two.

The Old Tavern

The tavern was old with a stale smell,
And the door didn't lock too well.

A stale smell of smoke and whisky,
Women dancing around being frisky.

Some women were for sale,
And others were there to drink the ale.

An old player piano played its tune,
It usually opened right around noon.

To this day, the old tavern still remains,
With whiskey running through their veins.

With spirits forgetting to move on,
The old tavern is still open till dawn.

The Pagan Priests

All lined up in long black clothes,
Watching the pagan witches pose.

Once a year, this ceremony takes place,
With the pagan witches in black lace.

Trying to choose their future wife,
To plan a long family life.

The pagan priests prepared for this,
And must choose one upon a kiss.

The Paranormal Museum

When walking into the dim lit room,
I hear sounds of laughter and doom.

Spirits that attached to their treasures,
Both big and small in different measures.

They attach themselves to something special,
You can feel it when you cross the threshold.

Dare enter the room of spirit past,
For fear of spells that can be cast.

I fear not the paranormal museum,
For I have met them all; I can see them.

The Raven

Black raven, what message do you have for me?
You flew into my window like you couldn't see.

The message must have been very profound.
You hit the window and fell to the ground.

Determined to warn me of a death to come.
That my mother was to lose her firstborn son.

You were sent by him of his death to be.
He passed at the time you came to me.

Oh, thank you, raven, for your angel wings.
You brought me comfort as I heard angels sing.

The Rocking Chair

Sometimes late at night, the chair would rock.
You can also hear some laughter and them talk.

Old rocking chair tattered, vintage, and broken.
So many nights I was awoken.

You haunt my chair with your spirit and sounds.
Rocking back and forth and moving all around.

The floor squeaks with age as you play your tune.
Rocking back and forth all night in my bedroom.

The Spirit Dance

The music played sweet and loving,
As couples danced while they were hugging.

It was a dance of many years ago.
They kept holding on and couldn't let go.

All the spirits danced across the room.
Still dancing and moving to the same tune.

Never to realize that they had passed.
Reminiscing the moments making them last.

Old dance hall of yesteryear.
This will always be a place to them so dear.

The Spirit of Alya

She is vibrant and beautiful with granting wishes.
She has a blue hue that's never vicious.

A genie spirit that is ancient from time,
With love and power, she'll fill your mind.

Alya's spirit has appeared in blue hue,
But she'll also manifest in full view.

When you call upon her, she's always there,
And will grant you a wish with care.

The Spring of Love

I remember it was a moon lit night in May,
As we watched the stars shining on the bay.

I didn't know it was our last night.
We made beautiful love in the moonlight.

We were only together from sunset till dawn,
Then it happened, and you were gone.

Like a riptide that washes up to the shore,
An angry sea that yelled with a roar.

I saw you adrift lifeless and pale,
As your boat had lost its sail.

The Storyteller

Once upon a time, I lived in a castle high on a hill.
I was a prince with power and permission to kill.

Brought before me to be judged and sentenced.
Never a chance to be forgiven with penitence.

I was the god who made the decisions.
Without any questions, options, or provisions.

Without any choice, I was sentenced to death.
Now I haven't any power or permission left.

The Tibetan Messenger

Messenger of the Tibetan gods with
his wisdom and insight.
He leaves messages under your
pillow when asleep at night.

Warnings to hear stories to tell answers to be given.
A messenger of God with words
to learn from heaven.

He moves strangely about the
room late in the night.
Searching for the answerers to
make sure they are right.

Guiding you to a dimension far
beyond your conscious thought.
His magic energy and intellect you
can only wish to be taught.

Embracing Tibetan messenger, I
keep you close at heart.
While I admire all your wisdom
and hope we never part.

The Time Traveler

We both know we loved before somewhere in time,
A familiar smile or maybe a meeting of the mind.

I'm familiar with your redemptions
and sins of your soul.
I know you much better than you
know your story told.

Don't look for me as I'm not visible to your sight.
You can't find me neither in the
darkness nor in the light.

I live within the depths of your
secret thoughts and mind.
I'm not your God, your Lucifer, or
your guest that you can find.

I'm all of you in motion, and you are me in part.
Close your eyes, and look down
deep into your heart.

See the light in the dark and shadows to be cast.
Somewhere before today you have lived in that past.

I know because I was there as a part of you.
We are both the same existence in all that we do.

Who are you, and what else do you want from me?
I thought for sure without a doubt,
I already set you free.

The Vixen

His love was blind and unconditional
And cared for her genuinely traditional.

Old-fashioned love he did profess,
But she in fact loved him less.

Sly and crafty took what she could
For money and riches is all she stood.

Then one day, she passed away,
But he still loves her to this day.

Sometimes, love has no eyes;
It comes to get you in disguise.

The Voices

It's you again; I recognize the
voice; I know who you are
Because I know myself well and
we seem to not be far.

Going up the staircase backwards
and falling down the hill,
You guide me wrong and make me
do all this against my will.

Voice of the night screams my name
in vulgarities and in hate;
You have become my friend in
both evil karma and in fate.

Don't touch me with that energy
nor think of me in lust,
For if you do, I shall revert my
soul and body back to dust.

You have no power as you think nor
do you control my mind;
Oh, I know your game of life, and
I'm familiar with your kind.

Are these voices in my head or
voices from the other side?
I guess that's my destiny and some
things we just can't hide.

The Voodoo Doll in the Wall

She sat in the wall for a long time
For the new owners soon to find.

Fixing the wall to make it new
Upon finding the doll of voodoo.

Ragged and dirty with a cloth face
Stuffed way back in a safe place.

A spell was cast to curse that old house,
But the people had moved out.

I summoned the spirit as I held the doll;
She said, "Please put me back in that wall."

The Walk-In

The walk-in spirit knew just what to do
Because it came within and made me new.

The walk-in spirits give new life
To dying souls that lose their fight.

Roaming the earth from the beginning of time
Trying to save souls that they find.

Giving life back where it was taken
Where all hope and life was forsaken.

The Well

It stands next to an old oak tree way up the hill;
Legend has it that children falling into were killed.

Some say from a distance, you
can still hear laughter;
Others say it's children's voices in the hereafter.

A woman said she saw an angel next to the well,
Yet another told of a story that chimed the bell.

A man saw two children playing near the well;
One was standing, and the other one fell.

Deep into the well, he went all the way down
Along with the other children that had drowned

The well still stands with its stories on the hill
As the angels watch, making sure no more are killed.

The Winding Road

It was a dark and misty cloudy sky;
The road was winding as we went by.

Twisting and turning going nowhere
Without any conscience not even a care.

An old man yelled, "Take a different turn!
Don't travel this road. There is nothing to learn."

"This road teaches only to the dead.
Take the alternate route just up ahead."

"Then wait for your turn next in line.
And I'll be there to greet you in time."

The Witches' Ball

Dressed in black, while some in white,
Dancing until the stroke of midnight.

The witches' ball comes once a year
Where they all gather in dance and cheer.

Balls always fall on a full moon
Valet parking for all their brooms.

And at the strike of the twelfth hour,
They must leave or lose their power.

I know all about their full moon balls;
I have attended some, just not all.

The Apparition

They appear in colorful hues of dark and light,
Without any preference of day or night.

Messages to give and stories to tell
Some from heaven and some from hell.

Needing to communicate with earthly souls
Hoping for answers yet to be told.

So when you experience a vision of unknown,
Always ask, "Who," in a friendly tone.

Tomorrow

Tomorrow I was born; yesterday I couldn't see;
Today, I called on my God and asked to talk to me.

With wisdom and love, the message came clear;
Today, I grew a person and now I can hear.

My mission, my assignment, and my growth within,
The masked charade of life is all it has been.

Is it my responsibility to bring happiness to you
Or is it shared together not as one but as two?

Am I good enough, am I pretty,
and am I smarter than you?
I'm happy I'm living these things you can't do.

Tomorrow is here I felt it go by;
Today is a thought of yesterday's lies.

Look at the moment, and live for the day;
If tomorrow was here, then today is to stay.

Fill your ears with wisdom; dry your eyes with sight;
Call upon your God, and look into the light.

If yesterday was gone and tomorrow
has already passed,
What does that leave you, and will it last?

True Love

Her body was lying in a pool of sweet sorrow
While waiting for that perfect tomorrow.

She loved with her heart that followed devotion
In giving her all in vows with emotion.

She's tattered and worn never to return
To many lessons and some not yet learned.

Wanting a love that will take her away
Holding on to a dream for another day.

Feeling her hurt while guarding her path
Wanting for true love and one that will last.

Until We Meet Again

Until we meet again, I will always love you;
You opened my heart, and gray skies became blue.

You touched me, and I knew I could still love;
You were like a special angel sent from above.

I loved your cute smile and your soft tender ways;
I still feel your kiss as though it's only been days.

I can hear your voice saying, "I
love you, oh, so much"
I still feel your presence and your
warm loving touch.

I miss you today and all days thereafter;
The fun we shared, the tears, and the laughter.

I know this kind of love is real and so true,
Knowing my heart will always belong to you.

Until we meet again, my heart has stood still;
Perhaps not this life but in another we will.

Voodoo Doll

I've sealed you in a little glass jar;
Put you on the shelf away and far.

You look at me with piercing eyes
And change your look in disguise

Sometimes you smile; sometimes you frown;
Sometimes I find you upside down.

You're haunted with a facetious spirit,
And at this point, you deserve no merit.

I can burn you in my witch pot today,
Or behave yourself if you want to stay.

When Dark Becomes Light

You summoned me to greet you
on a full moon–lit night
And asked me to take away your
darkness and show you to the light.

You said, "I've been lost for so long
and can't find my way"
I prayed to the full moon that night,
so you didn't have to stay.

I asked the gods to take you to a
place where you belong,
A place of light and peace with angels singing songs.

As I watch your spirit move with amazing grace,
I knew then and there you were in a safe place.

When the dark becomes light,
all angels sing in prayer;
They hold you tight and keep you
safe both here and there.

Oh, beautiful moon, what do you
behold for me tonight,
More spirits that need to be guided
to your luminous light?

White Witch of Salem

You visit often without my permission
And then depend upon my submission.

I'll summon you on the next full moon
And grant you wishes like flowers in bloom.

In abundance, you shall receive
Starting on the full moon's eve.

You come to me in white witch fashion
Wanting me to fill your passion.

White witch of Salem, I'm more powerful than you
In all that you want and more than you can do.

Wingless Angels

Angels of the earth with no wings
Having the power to change things.

Acting angels in disguise
Right before our very eyes.

Soft-spoken words with guiding light
Always there day or night.

So who's your angel without wings
That's there to help in many things?

Wise Buddha Man

He sits on the mantel quiet and strong
All day and all night long.

Messages from his wisdom within
His beliefs in richness and in sin.

Wise Buddha man teaches the path
And never to display anger or wrath.

I want to be more like him
With less to loose and more to win.

Wish Upon the Moon

Angels' and fairies' stardust and dreams
Drifting afar in a slumber of moon beams.

Jars filled with wishes, a pot full of gold
The moon and star secrets of the untold.

Oh, night becomes day, thoughts of sunshine
Behold, a beautiful color so warm and so kind.

Awaken the day, and welcome the night;
Wish upon the moon in its luminous light.

Yesterday Is Gone

I saw you today and held your
hand as you walked by;
No one was there just us, you and I, above the sky.

We journeyed together to a faraway dimension;
We kissed and said goodbye
without a word mentioned.

You went your way, and I found mine alone,
But something was missing; it wasn't home.

Yesterday is gone, and tomorrow happened today;
So what's here now is forever here to stay.

I'll miss you now and again this last time around,
But I'll always be looking for the
love that we once found.

Please take my hand again just one more time,
So that path will be there and not hard to find.

You Were There

The moon in the day, the sun in the night,
The stars in the eyes, the light for the sight.

The sound for the hearing, the touch for the feel,
The warmth for the heart, a soul waiting to heal.

The words left to speak, a thought for the day,
The tenderness of love in a sincere caring way.

The touch of a hand, the feel of an embrace,
The warm, tender words, the smile on your face.

The innocence of a child, the wisdom of the old,
The lifetime before one yet untold.

The passage of time, the hourglass sand;
The far reached out, and you touched my hand.

The darkness of the night no longer prevails,
Now only the sun and my secret love tales.

Your Smile

It's been a long time, now actually a while;
I have forgotten a lot but never your smile.

I still remember us back in the day;
You had to leave; I wanted you to stay.

Your God came and took you far away from me;
I can't remember much, but your smile I can see.

We did grow old together and were never apart;
Your smile will always remain deep in my heart.

Gods of Many

God, Buddha, Jehovah, and more,
We all pray to the same core.

Different names with many faces,
But when we die, we share their spaces.

Gods of different belief and name,
Some pray different; some pray the same.

Know your God, and trust in him;
Then you will be forgiven of sin.

Gods of many serve us the same;
He's just called upon with different names.

Lucifer Attends Church

Lucifer walked into the church in disguise;
God recognized him with his eyes.

God said, "Lucifer, I know you well,
Long before you lived in hell."

God said to Lucifer, "This is my home.
You left it for earth to roam."

"Come in peace, or leave now,"
And with that, Lucifer bowed.

Lucifer said, "You're king of this home.
I've just stopped by, and I'm all alone."

God looked at him, and He said,
"But I'm still alive; to me you're dead."

The Lost Ring

It's been years since she passed in the spring;
I have been looking everywhere for her ring.

Then one evening, I saw a beautiful light;
It was a sparkling wonderful sight.

I saw her face in the white hue;
Then I knew what to do.

I let it go, and then she smiled;
She said, "I'll see you in a while."

The Reunion

It wasn't a dream; it was too surreal;
Spirits gathered around I could feel.

Every family member and friend I knew,
Even some that were brand-new.

Including Aimée who was dancing about,
While others laughed, and some shout.

"A reunion from heaven, we're here to rejoice
Aimée has joined us; we heard her voice."

"We'll keep her safe and hold her near;
She has told us all about A. De Guerre."

"She's waiting for him by his side
To journey with him to be his guide."

Finding Aimée
A. De Guerre

The Roamers

They're all around you, walking about;
Some can see them coming in and out.

Earthbound spirits going places;
I can hear their voice without faces.

Talking in secret, sharing tales,
Some succeeded; others failed.

Meditate, and go deep into your soul;
Then find the stories to be told.

Aurora Borealis

Aurora Borealis, angels flying around;
These are special; they never touch the ground.

This is a home where they live;
Their wings are the light that they give.

Flying high and singing songs
Through the night and all day long.

Oh, special angels of that light
Showing off as they dance in flight.

Their beautiful messages are clear and loud
From some faraway place beyond our clouds

CPSIA information can be obtained
at www.ICGtesting.com
Printed in the USA
BVHW03s0958190718
522041BV00001B/29/P

9 781642 988765